7 Steps to Mastering Emotions

GAINING EMOTIONAL INTELLIGENCE & GETTING THE BEST OUT OF LIFE

JANIE CHARLOT, FNP-C

FAMILY NURSE PRACTITIONER

ISBN-13: 979-8-5897-1210-0

CONTENTS

From the Author

Dedication

1   Self-Mastery   1

2   Step 1- Identify Your Emotions   6

3   Step 2- Accept Your Emotions   9

4   Step 3- Analyze Your Emotions   12

5   Step 4- Choose How to Respond   14

6   Step 5- Know & Forgive Emotional Triggers   18

7   Step 6- See the Bigger Picture   21

8   Step 7- Take Action   24

Closing

About the Author

FROM THE AUTHOR

You were magnetically drawn to this book because you are ready to tap into the power within. You are done with suffering and want to live out your best life from the most powerful seat available to you- your authentic self! The first run through these steps may feel like a whirl wind. That's totally ok! These steps will require you to perhaps master one step before moving forward to the next. It may require you coming back to this book during many phases of your life as the best interpretation of life is experience. We can only gain self-mastery by gaining the knowledge and then applying it to our everyday lives. Besides, the application of knowledge is wisdom! As you master each step, be very proud of your progression. Be very confident to be mastering wisdom of the ages. Emotions are a topic we have suppressed for way too long. Maneuvering through this process can be scary- keep going anyway!

I sincerely hope that you will master each step of this book to unlock a life of freedom and empowerment. No longer do you have to go about life making the same mistakes and wondering why it keeps happening. We are all here to create the life of our dreams. We are creating every second of the day. Every single thing we can already see manifested in our lives, we created it! We are creating with our thoughts whether we are conscious of it or not. Our thoughts are creating our feelings (emotions). Our feelings are creating our words. Our words are creating our actions. Our actions are creating our patterns. Our patterns are creating our lives. Your emotions are alive within you! Like waves of water, they will rise and fall. Feeling the waves, keeps us alive. Becoming numb to them, is when we began to die. Master your emotions and have a smooth sail into the life you desire.

-Janie Charlot

DEDICATION

To the Most High GOD & All of Humanity

*"He who controls others may be powerful,
but he who has mastered himself is mightier still"*

— Lao Tzu

CHAPTER 1
SELF MASTERY

Why master our emotions? Well, we can genuinely connect to others and become more in-tuned with ourselves. We harness the power from within to create every experience we desire from the driver's seat. When we master our emotions and gain emotional intelligence we can motivate, inspire, and encourage others. Mastering our emotions stops the irrational responsiveness to the outside world, in which we cannot control; and connects us to the ever-expansive world within us, that we have full reign over. Truth is, if we cannot recognize the emotions in ourselves, it will be very difficult to recognize emotions in others. Most people believe everything that is happening to them is related to the environment or the circumstances surrounding them, but we are actually creating our own emotions that we feel!

I know this can be a strange concept to understand so I will further break it down. Let's say that I am fired from my job. I will most likely feel upset about this loss. I may feel a bit sad or rejected as well. If I get a compliment on my shirt, this compliment may make me feel happy, it may boost my self-esteem, and it can help me to feel good about myself overall. If I lose money on a bad investment, I may feel fearful as thoughts of how to replace the money lost begin to invade my mind. Feelings of lack and scarcity can also develop in this particular situation. If I start a new project, I may feel some anxiety because I am uncertain of the outcome. If I lose a loved one to death or end a relationship that I thought was going to last, I may feel depressed. I may even feel some lack, shame, loneliness, and doubt.

When we examine the above examples, we can see that there is a circumstance or a situation (loss of a job, compliment on a shirt, start of a new project, end of a relationship), and then there are the feelings regarding the particular circumstance (anger, sadness, happiness, joy, anxiety, lack, scarcity, depression, shame, doubt). It appears as if the circumstance and the emotions related to the circumstance co-exists. **However, we only feel certain emotions because of our THOUGHTS regarding the circumstance.** Let's continue to clarify. If I received a promotion at my job and I was expecting this to happen, then my emotions would most likely be neutral as I was already expecting the promotion. But if I received a promotion and was not expecting it, then I would feel a bit more excited because it came at a surprise.

To summarize the process, the external circumstance (job promotion) occurs, then our thoughts start to form in our mind regarding that particular circumstance (excitement or self-doubt). What is important to know is that the circumstance doesn't really hold any weight or value. A job promotion is just a job promotion. There are no emotions attached to it. However, our thoughts regarding the job promotion create the emotions that we feel towards it. **Therefore, our thoughts create our emotions. If this is clear, you can now understand how two different people can experience the exact same situation and come out**

of it with two totally different emotions and experiences of it.

Our thoughts go through a filter. This filter is often attached to the subconscious part of the brain and to our memory. Depending on particular memories in our brain, we may adopt particular emotions associated with those memories. The memory of a fatal car accident can bring up emotions of fear when triggered by driving past a certain stoplight. **If we can become AWARE of the memories or circumstances that are attached to certain emotions, we can truly master ourselves emotionally!** A daily awareness of our every thought is paramount in understanding how we are creating our own emotions, and therefore our own experiences.

Mastering this concept can truly afford a life of power over ourselves regardless of what could be happening around us. Emotional intelligence is not about manipulation. It is mastery over self, and not anyone else. It is gaining the necessary tools to feel, heal, and remain balanced. The following chapters will discuss the 7 steps to reaching this mastery.

"When awareness is brought to an emotion,

power is brought to your life"

-Tara Meyer Robinson

CHAPTER 2
STEP 1- IDENTIFY YOUR EMOTIONS

In order to gain mastery of our emotions, we have to actually identify what we are feeling. Commonly, people go about life "feeling" things but do not really know why, or even the source of their feelings. It is unhealthy and can be quite dangerous to dwell in a space of feelings and emotions and not know why. **To help identify emotions, we have to ask ourselves the following questions: What am I feeling right now? Why am I feeling this right now? Is there a root cause to this feeling that I have?** It is so important to ask these questions and truly seek the authentic answers within us. Our emotions are always communicating something to us. We just have to attentively listen!

The term depression is used very loosely, but is the

emotion really depression? Could it be loneliness and not depression? These two emotions can often show up the same way and feel the same way in the body. With loneliness, we may not want to go out by ourselves. We may want to just stay at home, and we may feel like we are alone in the world. Depression can show up the very same way. Sometimes anger shows up, and it's really hurt being masked. Truly taking time to identify what emotions we are feeling can be of greatest help in gaining mastery. **Without first identifying what we are feeling, we cannot begin to gain mastery over emotions.**

Do not be afraid of what you may find. Sometimes we identify that we have some repetitive emotional patterns that has been hidden in our blind spots. These repetitive patterns have been leading us either in the direction of the life we desire to create, or towards the mis-creations and falling just short of what we really want to happen. Either way, identifying your emotions, emotional patterns, and the impact it is currently having on your life is vitally crucial. Identification of emotional blind spots now brings forth that which is hidden, to light.

"All you really need to do is accept this moment fully. You are then at ease in the here and now, and at ease with yourself"

—Eckhart Tolle

CHAPTER 3
STEP 2- ACCEPT YOUR EMOTIONS

There is absolutely no way we can gain mastery over

our emotions by suppressing them. We have to accept

all that we feel. If I am starting a new project, feelings of

anxiety may surface because it's a new challenge that may

grow and stretch me. Once this anxiety is recognized, I can

begin to accept it. This anxiety can show up as fear, stress,

shortness of breath, and so many other stimulated

symptoms in the body. By recognizing and accepting it, I can

begin to work through the anxiety. I can call a dependable

friend that usually gives good emotional support. I can look

for ways to release the stress by taking a walk, listening to

soft music such as jazz, adapting techniques to slow down

breathing, incorporating a meditation regimen, or even just

writing my feelings out in a journal. **Accepting our emotions allows for healing. Some emotions can surface that are rooted in very painful experiences**.

Painful experiences are often suppressed as a protective mechanism. However, accepting fully how we feel about anything that happens in our lives allows for healing, learning, growth, expansion, teaching, forgiveness, and love to take place. **Suppressed emotions can show up in our physical bodies as weight gain, chronic illnesses, fatigue, lack of motivation, addictions, and a whole plethora of issues**. We attempt to fix the physical issue, never really un-veiling the emotional link. In this step, we come face to face in full acceptance of our emotions (good and bad). We open our own hearts up to loving ourselves through it. I do mean through it all- the joy and the pain. All the sides of ourselves we often keep hidden from others and the world; we begin to love all those parts at the deepest level. We nurture our own wounds in full knowledge that we have what it takes within us to do so. We do not need to seek anything outside of ourselves to feel loved or accepted at the deepest level.

"As you become more clear about who you really are, you'll be better able to decide what is best for you- the first time around"

-Oprah Winfrey

CHAPTER 4
STEP 3- ANALYZE YOUR EMOTIONS

Analyzing our emotions is when we become very curious about the emotions that are showing up. We become SELF-AWARE. We begin to see patterns in our emotional behavior and try to figure out the root cause. We may begin to seek out the input of those closest to us. We may take alone time in this step. The analyzing process will not occur over night. Allow yourself plenty of time with this process especially if there are deep negative patterns to discern and dissect. Perhaps you are now self-aware that you yell at your children a lot. When you begin to analyze why, you come to the realization that the root cause is frustration. You are overwhelmed at work, stressed to the max, and have been taking all of your frustration out on your children. **By analyzing our emotions, we can stop negative patterns and began to rectify them.** Be kind to yourself. When coming into new knowledge, we cannot judge our past choices as they were rooted in old beliefs.

"Forces beyond your control can take away everything you possess except one thing, your freedom to choose how you will respond to the situation"

-Victor Frankl

In this step, we consciously choose how we want to respond to outside situations. This requires emotional intelligence and emotional recognition in ourselves and others. **To make a choice, we must first be aware that we have options to choose from. We are becoming aware that we can actually choose our emotional responses.** Maybe you are a person that responds with anger. No matter the circumstance; your response is anger. You can be in traffic, and that angers you. Someone can tell you something, and that information causes you to respond in anger. You may hear something being said on television, that news triggers an angry emotional response.

This step requires us to intelligently observe our patterns. In this example, anger is the pattern. We can choose a different response such as patience. If you are in traffic, having patience with yourself and the other drivers will always serve you and others better. If someone tell you information that would normally anger you, choose understanding. Perhaps, ask more questions about the information being given before forming any conclusions. If you hear news on television that normally angers you, choose not to watch that particular program or get to a neutral emotion in response to it.

Consciously choosing our emotions gives us the POWER OVER OURSELVES. Emotions are energy in motion. We can halt that energy, allow it to simply flow through us by not responding at all, or we can transcend that energy. Transcending emotions is recognizing that a particular emotion may not be healthy at the moment. Transcending negative emotions is also choosing not to feed it by mirroring the same emotions back to others, but returning with a higher more positive emotion.

This step requires us to have patience with ourselves as we try to master it. This step will take time, practice, and a lot of self-awareness. Those angry traffic emotions will come up many times before you catch yourself and say "OK, I'm responding to this traffic with anger, it's a pattern, I should change this". You may be right in the middle of an emotional breakdown before it registers that you should choose a different emotion. **Just know that you can always stop, take a deep breath, and change up that emotion or energy in motion. You CAN CHOOSE to halt it or simply transcend it.**

"Self-care is knowing your emotional triggers & not surrounding yourself with energy that deliberately provokes them"

-Unknown

CHAPTER 6
STEP 5- KNOW & FORGIVE TRIGGERS

We are all emotional beings. We all have varied experiences, beliefs, personalities, likes, dislikes, and outlooks on life and living. **Emotional triggers can vary from person to person, and this makes us all unique. We become empowered when we know and are self-aware of our OWN triggers.**

Triggers can be people, places, memories, odors, events, words, seasons, music, etc. You can walk into a place and it can trigger some type of emotion. A battered wife can easily have painful memories triggered simply by hearing her abusive husband's name. Maybe each time you smell the scent of a certain perfume, an emotion is triggered in memory of your loving grandmother. Loving memories will always comfort us and grant us peace in needed times. It's the painful memories that can keep us emotionally paralyzed and on the hamster wheel of emotional toxicity. Know your emotional triggers and avoid them.

Forgiving emotional triggers is learning how to detach from them. It is coming into the knowledge that perhaps that place or that person was a trigger in the past. **However; at this step, you have done all the necessary inner work.** Now, that person or that place may no longer have you responding to it in the same way you once did. When you can authentically get to this place emotionally when faced with triggers, you have detached and have gained mastership over this step.

"When you change the way you look at things, the things you look at change"

-Wayne Dyer

CHAPTER 7
STEP 6-SEE THE BIGGER PICTURE

To master our emotions, we have to see the bigger picture! When we get overwhelmed with lower emotions of anger, sadness, anxiety, or depression we can easily get hyper focused on the current situation. But if we take time to broaden our view and perspective, it can prevent us from drowning in our own despair.

Understand that when unexpected situations occur in our lives, it's always happening FOR us, and not to us. Unforeseen circumstances occur to grow and expand our beliefs. It is to help us evolve into the better version of ourselves. If we do not see the bigger picture and act in the moment, we can potentially do something that cannot be undone. These are the snap situations we hear and read about. In the heat of emotions, snap decisions are made and severe consequences can occur. Sometimes the life of another is taken under these highly charged emotional states.

Take a step back and see the bigger picture. **Ask yourself these questions: The emotion I am feeling right now, will I care about this in 24hrs? Will I care about this situation in another year from this moment? Will this emotion serve the better version of myself in the next five years? How will this emotion serve me once it fades?**

"All human actions are motivated at their

deepest level by one of two emotions–Fear or Love"

–Unknown

CHAPTER 8
STEP 7- TAKE ACTION

The last step is taking action. This is when we are being proactive and we are actually transforming our emotions and taking control on a daily basis. Our actions are illustrating that we have gained mastership over our own emotions. **We are not responding to our outside environment, but dictating the environment for ourselves.** At this stage we can walk into the office of another, take note of the energy in the room, and authentically know that no matter what is going on in that particular office, we have control over our own internal environment. We are taking this kind of action in all facets of our lives: inside our homes, with our children, in the workplace, and with all whom we externally come in contact with. We are setting the emotional tone for ourselves in all that we do. We have internalized that all peace, joy, happiness, and love come from within regardless of what we may or may not physically be experiencing around us. Most importantly, we can TRANSFER this same peace, joy, happiness, and love that we have harnessed within ourselves into the lives of all those around us because it comes from the most authentic place- Within. And when we go within, we have tapped into an infinite amount of resources available to us to fulfill every desire we could ever dream.

CLOSING

The life you desire awaits you! As spiritual beings having a physical experience called life, we must maintain the harmony and balance of all parts of ourselves: physical, mental, and spiritual. Your emotions are at the root of all 3 parts and can have a major impact on all of them. You get to choose if it will be a positive or negative impact- and this makes you powerful! You are a powerful creator! Adding emotions to our heart's desires provides fuel for faster manifestations. I just highly recommend making them of purest intent and for the greater good of all. We are more than our external circumstances. We are more than falling prey to thought patterns that do not serve the life we really want to live. Our emotions are here to communicate to us and work with us, do not drown them out! Much Love & Light as you utilize these steps and incorporate them into your daily living for the most purpose filled experiences.

ABOUT THE AUTHOR

Janie Charlot is A Family Nurse Practitioner, founder of Matters of the Heart & Soul Podcast, and Founder of NP's Hired Health & Weight Management Clinic. She is a lecturer, transformational coach, and author of several publications. She was raised in Church Point, LA and currently resides in Atlanta, GA. Visit her website at www.nphired.com.

Printed in Great Britain
by Amazon

44176876R00020